the road north

Ken Cockburn (1960–) is a poet and translator based in Edinburgh. After studying French and German at Aberdeen University, and Theatre Studies at University College Cardiff, he worked for several years with touring theatre companies in Wales. He later worked as Fieldworker for the Scottish Poetry Library, taking the library van to schools, libraries and community centres across Scotland. He and Alec Finlay established and ran pocketbooks, publishing 16 books taking a 'contemporary and generalist view of Scottish culture' (1999-2002). He has worked freelance since 2004, regularly collaborating with visual artists including Mary Bourne, David Faithfull and Andrew MacKenzie. His published translations include poems by Christine Marendon, Arne Rautenberg and Thomas Rosenlöcher. Recent publications include *Ink*, with artists ~in the fields (2011), and *Overheard Overlooked: Found Poems* (2012). www.kencockburn.co.uk

Alec Finlay (1966–), artist and poet, lives and works in Edinburgh. Working across a wide range of media and forms, including microtonal installations, sculpture, mapping and journeys, books, print works, and audio-visual, much of Finlay's work considers how we as a culture, or cultures, relate to landscape and ecology. He was the first AiR at BALTIC, and has exhibited at the Sydney Biennale. Recent artist projects include *Sweeney's Bothy*, an artist-residency hut for the Isle of Eigg, and Taigh, Scotland's national memorial for organ and tissue donors, installed in Edinburgh's Royal Botanic Garden. Among his recent poetry collections are *Be My Reader* (2012), *A Company of Mountains* (2013), *today today today* (2013), and *a-ga: on mountains* (2014). He is represented by Ingleby Gallery and publishes artist blogs at www.alecfinlay.com

Some other publications by Ken Cockburn

Souvenirs and Homelands
The Order of Things: an anthology of Scottish sound, pattern
   and concrete poems (edited, with Alec Finlay)
The Dancers Inherit the Party: Early stories, plays & poems
   by Ian Hamilton Finlay (edited)
Intimate Expanses: XXV Scottish Poems 1978-2002
   (edited, with Robyn Marsack)
The Season Sweetens / Die Saison Versüssend: Football Haiku 2006
For "visions" read "meteors": found poems, and an alphabet, from the
   John Murray Archive
Feathers & Lime: translations from the German
On the flyleaf
CENTUM: 100 Years of Baillie Gifford 1908-2008 (with David Faithfull)
Overheard Overlooked: found poems
Ink (with ~in the fields)
Snapdragon: poems by Arne Rautenberg (translated)
While yet we may

Some other publications by Alec Finlay

Ludwig Wittgenstein: There Where You Are Not (with Guy Moreton
   & Michael Nedo)
siren (with Chris Watson)
Two fields of wheat seeded with a poppy-poem (with Caitlin DeSilvey)
Nose's Point: a coastal walk (with Thomas A. Clark)
Specimen Colony (with Jo Salter)
One Hundred Year Star-Diary (with Denis Moskowitz & Ray Sharples)
Mesostic Remedy (with Laurie Clark & Linda France)
Mesostic Interleaved (with Ken Cockburn)
Ian Hamilton Finlay: Selections (edited)
A Company of Mountains
Question Your Teaspoons
today today today
Thorns
Sweeney on Eigg
a-ga: on mountains (with Ken Cockburn & Luke Allan)

Ken Cockburn
& Alec Finlay

the road north

*a journey through Scotland
guided by Bashō's* oku-no-hosomichi
15 May 2010 – 15 May 2011

Shearsman Books

First published in the United Kingdom in 2014 by
Shearsman Books
50 Westons Hill Drive
Emersons Green
BRISTOL
BS16 7DF

Shearsman Books Ltd Registered Office
30–31 St. James Place, Mangotsfield, Bristol BS16 9JB
(this address not for correspondence)

www.shearsman.com

ISBN 978-1-84861-358-4

Copyright © Ken Cockburn & Alec Finlay, 2014.
The right of Ken Cockburn & Alec Finlay to be identified as the authors
of this work has been asserted by them in accordance with the
Copyrights, Designs and Patents Act of 1988.
All rights reserved.

Acknowledgements
The references to Bashō's *Oku-no-hosomichi* are from the translation by
Cid Corman and Kamaike Susumu, *Back Roads to Far Towns*.

*Cover image: Alec Finlay & Tomohiko Ogawa, photograph Tomohiko Ogawa,
2010. (The original image has been reversed.)*

Contents

I	Setting out	9
II	First Views of the Foothills	
	what is a journey?	17
	Bonnington House & Jupiter Artland	18
	Maspie Den & West Lomond	22
	Falkland	24
	Kingskettle	26
	The Hermitage, Dunkeld	27
III	Our Shirakawa	
	Perthshire glens	31
	Dalchonzie	33
	Sma' Glen	34
	Newton	35
	Acharn	36
	Ken's Dunira	37
	Alec's Dunira	39
	Saint Fillan's Hill	40
IV	Beyond the Border-line	
	tanzaku	45
	Glen Lyon	46
	what is a glen?	47
V	Archaic Argyll	
	what is a cup-&-ring marked rock?	51
	the hollow marks…	52
	sun's not shifted	53
	what is a dun?	54
	Dunadd	55
	Loch Etive	56
	Annie Briggs	58

VI	Rocks & Peaks	
	mountains without end	61
	what is a mountain?	62
	casting our chosen peaks	63
	Schiehallion	65
	Outlandia	67
VII	Woods & Glens	
	woodland credo	71
	Loch Eilt	72
	Loch Eilt rite	73
	the Glenelg brochs	74
	Abhainn a' Ghlinne Bhig, Glenelg	76
VIII	Westerly Shores	
	Matsushima / Luing	79
	what is a beach? what is the sea?	80
	Isle of Luing	81
	Moidart, Arisaig and Morar	82
	Dun Scaich	84
IX	The Outer Isles	
	ding-dong, ding-dong	87
	Lochmaddy	88
	Barpa Langais	89
	Berneray	92
X	Crossing into Autumn	
	Slioch	97
	The Groves of Isle Maree	98
	River Inverianvie	100
	Glen Etive	103
XI	Winter Interned	
	Sora's illness	107

XII Weak March Sun
    what is a hut?   111
    Carbeth   112

XIII Spring Paths, Summer Opening
    what is faith?   115
    St Medan's Cave & Chapel   116
    Acharn Falls   118

XIV Epilogues
    Alec's Epilogue   123
    Ken's Epilogue   125

Appendix   129
Notes & Acknowledgements   132

I

Setting Out

so, when was it
I first had that dream
of roving the glens
up and down
guided by Bashō's Oku?

some morning
I will wake on Pillow Hill
with a matinal willow
warbling at the window
books on the bed
my heart in a fankle

to see clouds and mountains
in the far-away
to be on the road north
where paths of moss and crottle
follow peaty waters

some morning I will cross over
to the Kingdom
shrouded in mist
tracking back
to the origin of things
sipping tea from a shell

I will learn how to tell
burns that run
lochan to lochan
from the wide river
that flows freely
to the sea

I will turn down
some other glen
east-west into low sun
scooping shelter
from a mountain wind
to plant two rowans

by a white croft
waiting for a boy
whose supple hand
will gently twist
the pliant saplings
so they grow entwined

ten years on
pink again in the park
and a flitting
in the offing
as I swap one view
for another

familiar streets

   Pilrig
   Rosslyn
   Bonnington

exchanged for hills

   Lomond
   The Buachaille
   Roshven

it's time to pack

old pink and new orange maps
a picnic blanket for the dog
yellow bottles of Rescue Remedy
miso packets, rice noodles,
oatcakes, flasks and chocolate

compass, gazetteers, pens
pencils for rubbings
wee Moleskine notebooks
hokku-labels for trees
and paper wishes

a handful of CDs

Neil Young's Jukebox
Anne Briggs
Dylan's 'Highlands'

mind the teas

Iron Warrior
Monkey on the Mountain
Black Ruby
Gabalong
Grasshopper Oolong

and the whiskies

Glenkinchie
Tullibardine
Bruichladdich
An Cnoc
and the Super Nikka!

come summer we'll name our band

   shafts of sun

come fall we'll name our album

   bands of rain

now we're leaving behind
lanes of gean
blossoming in The Meadows
heading off on the *hosomichi*
to look for Shirakawa

now we'll let our looking
survey Scotland
from Monreith to Poolewe
setting out to see
the best view
of all where the land
meets the sky

II

First Views of the Foothills

what is a journey?

a journey is the day
it's impossible
to stay

the day *there*
means more
than *here*

the day you
enter the view
from your window

our beginning is a walk
at Jupiter Artland, Bonnington House, West Lothian

far over the Firth
north through the thin
line of pale ash
over the pommel
of Binny Craig
noble Illieston
the pinkish bings
of Albyn, Faucheldean, Greendykes
relic spoil turning green

the Forth's strutting span
of rivet and iron
Mossmorran's fractionated cloud
lifting above Bishop Hall
and domed West Lomond

today we can see
to where we'll meet ourselves
next week up by the Yad

blackthorn winter
should be over now
but there's a fresh
sprinkling of snow
on East Cairn
reckoning by the old ways
it's Mayday
and Bashō's anniversary
so let's bawm the thorn
with the riches of rags

each morning I end my walk
at the wood's edge
with the silver selvage
of a copper beech,
its tight buds
tense to open

who'd have thought it
there's cones
under those pines
just waiting for
some warmth
to split scattering
their seed

brushing my fingers
a drift of white
softly flowers
on the earthy stump
as wood-sorrel
bitter as should be
by the bracken that
uncurls viol scrolls
and makes fronds
with the prickly rasp

they share the shelter
of the old quarry's
stern rock edge

rusting nearby is
the double-barrel
of Parker's resting gun

on the font of the wood
is Finlay's sun temple
dedicated to

that wild red youth,
Apollo-Saint-Just, incarnate
forging a revolution
from the whole
framed in the round
by the cupola
that highlights azure
in the changeless
ever-changing sky

our first hill gives the first view of the oku *to come*
on a walk up Maspie Den & West Lomond, Kingdom of Fife

the sky's chosen
to fall in on
Onesiphorus' temple
but today's not the day
to stop and listen
to the echo of ruin

up the Yad's single thread
the douce wee pools say

   after you – no, after you

beyond Craigmead
the path taken looked
not to advance at all

the volume of birdsong's
steady then
slightly hazy at the top
I can't see my way
back over the Forth
scan the yellow patches

stitched on the Howe's
undulating cloth
name the dead

   Susan C. Mackay

   3-11-82
   18-8-95

the path snakes
through skylarks
primroses in flower
unripe blaeberries
I'll come back with the kids
when they're ready

*Bashō's Ueno
is Sonia's orchard*

*cupped in the hollow
at the centre of it all*

leaving behind olives
almonds and peaches
Sonia found herself
this cottage garden
and northern view

settling down snug
where the heir of air
is flecked by blossom
falling in pinches
she'll soon sow

> *yarrow
> button-headed scabious
> moon-rayed oxeye
> lady's smock
> lilac with a liking for
> the Maspie's damp*

she never forgets
the winter prune
perched up the ladder
shaping a canopy
of cropped Ys

she's added a millennial
scattering of natives
to the old commercials,
small stunted *malus*
with nary a petal to shed

Forfar
Early Julyan
Lass o' Gowrie
The Bloody Ploughman
White Paradise

tea and cake with Ella, at Kingskettle

(i.m. Tom McGrath)

at Ash Villa
passenger trains are short
goods trains long

*if a blackbird
comes to join us
that'll be Tom*

a walk to The Hermitage, Dunkeld

Even their hesitation was tinged with heroism…

I hunt the rushing sound
through dark stands of pine
finding the river
where the arch
of the old stone bridge
straddles the angry Braan
and I marvel at the lads
on the parapet
grazed by rays
of Ossianic sun
one about to dive in

&
about
to dive
in

&
still
about
to
dive

&

&

&

III

Our Shirakawa

anticipation each day mounting…

*we were guided toward Shirakawa
through green Perthshire glens*

*if you're travelling
in the north country fair,
where the wind hangs heavy
on the border-line…*

people ask us the way
to the Shirakawa Barrier
and we reply, take it easy,
the Shirakawa Barrier
is everywhere

the map's watershed
is Shirakawa,
reading the names of
burns running south-east
allts flowing north-west

lovers' beeches'
gully-carved hearts and initials
are Shirakawa,
an intimacy
between settlement
and elsewhere

Comrie's confluence of
Lednock, Earn and Ruchill
is Shirakawa:
Edo to the east
in the orderly market-town,

oku to the west
in twilit deer, pheasants
lacking road-sense,
tumbledown gardens
and close-ranked pines

any wee road
where your fingers
brush meadowsweet verges
is Shirakawa,
when you let the wheel turn
through the glen
with all your attention
on the encounters and minor
dramas of PAS-
SING PLACES

any one-street village with
shops stocking FANCY GOODS
and a butcher's that sells
a new brand of oatcakes
is Shirakawa

any clicked latch
of a gate that
makes a space
for things to come
is Shirakawa

Dalchonzie is Shirakawa

the tailrace
is still as
a mirror pool

Sma' Glen is Shirakawa

the green glen
is an upturned bell
cast between Meall Tarsuinn
and Dùn Mòr,
with the great Stone its clapper

scratch-marks on the face
of Clach Ossian
are they from ice or flame?
now tell me
who moved this erratic
to make the grave?

*Newton, where we stopped for a pee
and happened on the beeches, is Shirakawa*

the fanks are empty of sheep
brought down from Dalmore,
Creag Chruinn, Alpinishields

while the herd's dipped or clipped
shepherd lads while the time away
singing and signing
nadokoro bark

a carved comet flares
over the gash of

   1 8 6 0

bright when the trees
were young

Acharn is Shirakawa

gazing up from Loch Tay's
wide shingle shore
to the slopes of Ben Lawers,
knowing they're surely
laced with midsummer's
alpine wildflowers

the white cottage, Drum na Keil, Dunira
is where Ian Hamilton Finlay lived after the war;
he is our monk Kashin,
and the walk to the cottage is Ken's Shirakawa

"I loved my shed at Drum na Keil,
its tarred, leaky roof,
the wee windows full
of mountains and pines…"

unlike children, the hunters
are heard but not seen
as one June evening
I follow the track

through woods and unfenced meadows
climb by the storied burns
towards 'Finlay's Cottage'
not knowing if it's inhabited

beyond a telephone-mast
making out as the fakey fir
I find it trim and whitewashed
but no-one's in

bottles ranged on the long
table maybe the
invisible hunters
will return to later

I'm almost back when
a circle of tall trees
draws me into what's left
of a formal garden

fluted columns
picturesquely
toppled into deep-
ening grasses

wide stone steps
mossy and burst
by a sycamore
and a balustrade

so colonised by
bramble and vine
it's hard to see
what's beyond

here there is no
canopy of sail
to break the horizon
of *Mare Nostrum*

*Alec's Shirakawa is an evening walk from The Square,
Dunira, to the great sycamore, which is our great chestnut
at Sukagawa, the one Bashō says Tokyu would sit under*

from behind tilted pine
a last ray of sun
fans over The Square,
it lifts my shadow
through the wooden rails,
fetches it far ahead of me

under the great sycamore
a darker green
cools the evening,
the deer browse mist
floating leglessly, seeming
to sense my looking

lifting their heads
then leaping the fence
they fade into the wood,
beyond shafts of light
that pick out wisps
on the dying branches

Saint Fillan's Hill is Shirakawa

that dumb saint
that splendid mute
was never one
to set himself over
the higher peaks

head pillowed west
his seat gifted meaning
to the hills' outline
giving this conspectus view

clamber up the scree field
fringed by toxic foxgloves
or go by stonecrop's stars
snug in veins of dry rock

lying among bluebells
feet pointing east
the saint's seat looks north
toward the confluence

I aim my arm
down Glen Artney
the glen of pebbles

along the ridge
of Bealach Ruadh
the ruddy pass

to the picturesque crown
of Mòr Bheinn the great peak

IV

Beyond the Border-line

I wind a few words
round the stalks
of plaited bog-grasses

and green rushes
hooking the knot
over the spike

pulling the bow tight
on the seed-head
aiming the camera

at *tanzaku* left among
catkins and the leaves
of alder and rowan

to be found
and undone
whether from love

or disliking
or left for the sun
and rain
to seasonally fade them

where, or when,
there was nothing
to be said
we folded the taper
of a paper wish

around a branch
silently saying over
the names of the dead

and the living
who are bravely
doing their dying

*Bashō's Michinoku
is our longest glen, Glen Lyon,
surrounded by the Heart's Mountains*

on the longest day
we slip in by Sput Ban
looking for the Lyon

along crooked Gleinn Fasach,
the deserted glen,
the glen of stones,
where once twelve castles strode

tides of nettles thrive
in Carbane's ruined hearth,
at each corner

the rowan will flame
remembering the flight
of the arrow

slow in lithe waters
we turn our strokes
upstream, towards

the stone family
washed and set
before the doorway of
Taigh na Caillich

what is a glen?

air where once
there was ice

heather where once
there were trees

wind where once
there was breath

V

Archaic Argyll

what is a cup-&-ring marked rock?

a cup-&-ring marked rock is

a monolithic map
of we know not what

a megalithic board-game
whose rules are lost

a petrified ripple

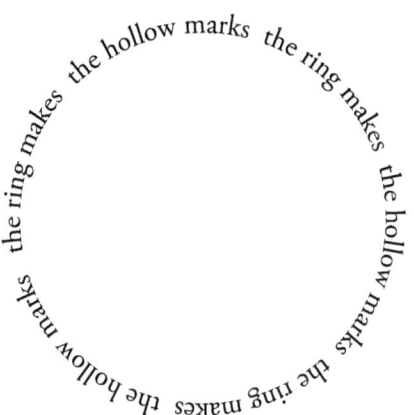

sun's not shifted

seeing light

leaves beneath

dark trees

lichens drift

grey waves

lifting clouds

closed shadows

nodding foxglove

meadowsweet

clustered hazel

pine fan open

puckered fern

pecked stone

cupped star

ring   stone   bone

stone quern

pockled rock

wetted vein

pooled moss

what is a dun?

a dun is
the lowest point
you can see
everything

a walk to Dunadd

picture the dun as it was
islanded by tides that
erase the Add's meanders

washing over Moine Mhor's
bricolage of moss & rush
patched heather pools
and cloud shadows

mount the split hill
or shapely paps
let the right
foot in

*Bashō's Mount Gassan
is our Loch Etive and her mountains
where we imagine Deirdre's waterfall
and her Tigh Grianan, or sun-bower*

we've scanned the maps
read up the old stories
now Donald phones to say
our approach from the south

 a cruise on Scotland's most beautiful sea loch!
 Seating for 12
 Teas & Snacks

is cancelled by today's rain

the loch bends deep
between the mountains
towards the glen's fastness

the secret sun-bower
we'll seek next month
and dream today

Deirdre and Naoise
exiles happy a while
in the badlands

as trees on steeps
thrive beyond
the deer's reach

as berry-laden rowans
sheltered in the gorges
cling with sturdy roots

as birches gusts
bend and harry
mint leaves of gold

forced to depart
when the game fails
Ulster brings only sorrows

and they return as swans
a muted assembly
at Camas na Cùirte
Bay of the Court

the rain hasn't stopped
but, ach, we're brighter
out here in the wild

*Bashō's old recluse called Tosai at Fukui
is our Annie Briggs and her garden at Kilmiddlefern*

*his yugao, hechima, keito and hahakigi
her sunflowers, bugloss, weld and gourds*

the piping so lost her
when he asked her name
she was beyond knowing
she'd ever had one
– but she knew to reply

*Willie Clancy, let me
sing you a song
then I will find my name*

that last harsh frost
stayed the longest
stealing the blossom
from the plum

but in Annie's garden
nectarines ripen
against the warmth
of the wall

grown from a stone
carried from the old
Tea-Garden at the end
of the track to Gylen

VI

Rocks & Peaks

these are our mountains without end

Bashō's Nikko
is our Slioch

Bashō's Kurokami
is our Ben Lawers

Bashō's Shitomae
is our Beinn Dorain

Bashō's Haguroyama
is our Schiehallion

Bashō's Gassan
is our Ben Cruachan

Bashō's Chokai
is our Dùn Caan

Bashō's Shirane
is our Grianan nam Maighdean

Bashō's Hina
is our Cuillin

what is a mountain?

a mountain is what you go a long way round to avoid

a mountain is a walk into the unknown

a mountain is the crazy river's reason

a mountain is what's not worth having

a mountain is identified by its thumbprint of contour lines

a mountain is nothing without its skyline

a mountain is a zone of intransigence

a mountain can't even recall its own name

a mountain is where we realise how far short we fall of the birds

a mountain is where even the scouring glaciers had to admit defeat

a mountain is the last resort of extreme views

casting our chosen peaks
before our eyes
we've stood here

long enough
to face our rain
now it's time

to tuck our boot-
socks in and begin
forcing the lines

you climbed
and you climbed, Ken!
Ach, how you climbed!
and how I would have liked
to join you!

Up there where the Allt Mor
spills and gurgles,
up there where I can't go,
up where the sun's shining

And even if I can't get
to where Big Eck
seems to be pointing,
into that far patch of green
marking the hillside spring
from which the fawn leaps
and the last cairn,
where the cup
of wound's
securely chained,
then I can still
lie here weighing
the lag in my legs

Ach, there's nothing for it
but to take a leaf
from my dear Jo
and fall asleep,
dreaming Schiehallion,
dreaming Lushan's moon
afloat on Dunalastair's silver screen

these are the heart's mountains
Bashō's Haguroyama
our Schiehallion

beyond trees
beyond bracken and heather
beyond ruined farms
beyond inlaid stone steps
beyond way-cairns
beyond false summits
beyond the ankle-wrenching boulder-field
beyond cloud

I offer the topmost cairn
a cube of white quartz
chosen on the lower slopes
and the angel's share
of the Tullibardine
a midsummer toast

    Schiehallion! Schiehallion! Schiehallion!

look out on implausible
rows and rows
of flown-in peaks
the sheen of Lochs
Tummel and Rannoch
and descending
after my shadow
I see everything
in a new light
bog cotton
the waxing moon
dribbles of white
through the rock

height in my ears
at the foot
the gloaming trembles
with rowan-blossom

a walk to a view of snowy peaks, Outlandia, Glen Nevis

out the single window
the Ben leans in
over the poet's
rude desk and chair
gazing up at snowy peaks

there's folk over there
hiking up the gully
– hey, why not play
our new game

PAPER—CLOUD—MOUNTAIN

CLOUD
  obscures
    MOUNTAIN

      PAPER
       absorbs
        CLOUD

         MOUNTAIN
        pulps
          PAPER

VII

Woods & Glens

this is our woodland credo

reach for the light
but keep a strong centre
to blow about in storms

be airborne as rowan
which occur farther off
than bird-shat birches

be windcast as alder
by floating downstream
or blowing up the burn

be hybrid as larch
cast from a cannon
onto steep slopes

learn from the pine
be first to shed
your old needles

cling to the trunk
or climb branch-
over-branch
up there where
the canopies
pull-out their pockets
filling the air
with birdsong

a walk and a swim, Loch Eilt

*when will the boat take me
to the pines of Shiogoshi?
when will I 'build me a cabin
in the mountains so high'?*

we're close now
to the western sea
tethered near a jetty
and a NO FISHING sign
is our blue boat

the Mallaig train
passes magically close
to Eilean Mor and Eilean an Tighe
where relict trunks
still grow tall

for no northerly
can squeeze through
the birch notch
of the Mhuidhe
to chill the sheltered slope

many milky torrents
feed Loch Eilt
deep as they are
these burns know nothing
of the tides ebbing
just a glen away

    Allt a Choire Bhuidhe   *burn of the yellow corrie*
    Allt Easain   *burn of the waterfall*
    Allt Dearg   *the red burn*
    Allt Raineachan   *bracken burn*
    Allt na Criche   *burn of the heart*

time for a skinny-dip

we find our own
wee gravel beaches,
each just big enough for
   one

such places charm,
inviting an act, a rite
done right
and so to sipped

tea and whisky,
labels and wishes
we've added the
sporadic plunge

a loch, a jetty,
the allure of a boat

   Erailort

and we're no' daft
– a dozen strokes there
chittering teeth clenched
tight for a snap
– *sea*-cold, not *river*-cold –
a dozen strokes back

but it's the tops,
it's the Pass o' Brander,
it's the tops,
it's a diving goosander

and the air
suddenly warmer
when we re-emerge

a walk to the Glenelg brochs
Dùn Grugaig, Dùn Troddan, Dùn Telve
broch-of-the-queen – and one each for her sons?

each broch's
a sounding chamber
portioning the river's babble
so let's roll Gleann Beag
up the Balvraid cow-track

is it there then
hid in the trees?
we've to gauge Grugaig
by following Iosal
down to the bend

the curved walls hint at
the twinned shell bottle-form
roof-beams at a height
my confused imagination
can't return

Troddan's stepworn cross-
sectioned scarcements
and slabbed lintels
rimmed with melancholy
thistles & pale grasses

Telve still bending
its trim tower
below Cùl an Dùin
each stone runs
the river farther on

over the glen
the hidden burn's shown
in a paper-tear of trees

alder, willow, rowan, hazel

threading a soft vein
through the spruce regimen

these broken crowns
hidden by docks and nettles
thought's full of gaps
ground to chaff
in the broken quern

so close your eyes
and cover the wall-
tops with eaves
adding the bustle that flickers
round a big fire

shall we go then,
to the ends of Glenelg
whose name flows
both ways?
as the river grades
shingle hoards
around each bend
sorted for ease

by spates that braid
rich films of alluvium,
marginalia whetting
a fine solution
for the banks,
on down the strath
back to Eilanreach,
across the kyle

to the island hills
and the dark crotch
of wood between Sgùrr
na Coinnich and Ben Aslak,
rippling at a run
the river has no idea
how its mouth
swells and fans

for the final breach
where it gushes
into the mineral stream,
flushes beyond
the pebble strand,
where pure water
is ceaselessly broken
on the briny fret

VIII

Westerly Shores

Bashō's Matsushima, all sorts of islands gather here, steep ones pointing to sky, others creeping upon waves ... some piled double on each other, or even triple, and some divided at one end and overlapping at the other

is our Jura, Scarba, Lunga, Fiola Mheadhonach, Rubha Fiola, Eilean Dubh Mòr, Eilean Dubh Beag, Ormsa, Fladda, Belnahua, Garbh Eileach, Dùn Chonnuill, A' Chùli, Eileach an Naoimh, Dubh-fhèith, Easdale and the Ross of Mull, seen from Luing

Bashō's Ojima Beach
is our Sandaig

Bashō's Shiogama
is the red sands
at Little Gruinard

Bashō's bay called Nago
is our Camus Gaineamhaich
where the Inverianvie meets the sea

Bashō's Iro Beach
is our Singing Sands at Ardnish

what is a beach?

a beach is an abacus
which counts in lines
powered by the moon

what is the sea?

if the sea knew what
it was it wouldn't
keep coming back

a view from the Isle of Luing, our Matsushima

islands upon islands
shattering into countless fragments
the summer sea

we're helped to see farther
looking through Edna's
pencil-scratched
paper-tearing storms

she says she could

take away that building
but I've learnt
to look through it

seeing the sun shining
through the back of my head
by the sunset
out the back window

*A squeaking walk on the singing sands
of Moidart, Arisaig and Morar*

it's another day
to walk the strand
on Rubha Dà Chuain
where every cap
could be a seal flipping

another day
to look south
for the lost wind
which will open the bay
to gentler weather

another day
when our shell-cult holds sway
in Chonzie's crown of razors
tucked in the fold
of his *Thinsulate* hat

another day
to sip dark tea
from the mussel's flared rim

another day perfection
dulls the shore's zonation
as we squeak the fine
white sands of Morar,
their dead silica so clean

another day to finger poems
for the tide to read
and erase

another day
of salt water
without storm,
light shattering
glinting fragments

another day
the sea reaches deep
spray falls
and orange-shanked
littoral birds want mud

another day
it's all unfolding
under the fucoid wrack
quieting the dark
tidal wood

a walk to Dùn Scaich, Sleat, Isle of Skye

Bashō's Tsuruga
is Tarskavaig
where we visited Meg

his *wild geese at Mt. Kaeru*
are the wild geese crying over the waves
of Òb Ghabhsabhaig

his *reeds at Tamae*
are the spaghnum bogs, milkwort
and bog-cotton of Tokavaig

his *Castle of Hiuchi*
is Dùn Scaich
with cliff-top rowan
and void drawbridge

IX

The Outer Isles

ding-dong, ding-dong
this is Caledonian MacBrayne
serving the Western Isles

it's brisk out here
taking in the Minch
from the rails of a Cal-Mac
eyes peeled for basking sharks

seeing the way the blocks
of the world
hug each other
and brush up
against each other

their weight
their air
their colour
and the soft uncertain
spaces between them

an evening walk, Lochmaddy, North Uist

just for once
the big wings
of the wind
are taking a rest
while we walk
in the dark
collecting a different moon
in each finger of lochan

constant in phases
the incremental moon
gets a good washing
in the waves
rippling its broad beam,
tickling the waves,
silvering the pixils
of the Gaelic ocean

Bashō's Eiheiji temple
'a thousand li from Hoki'

is Barpa Langais,
our chambered cairn
on North Uist

we turn Langais deasil
following the sun's
right way, looking
skew north to Marrogh's cairn
over the weft
of deer-grass and moss

to the gash in the wood
where it surrendered
to the will of the wind,
as the sea-breeze
picks up handfuls,
or armfuls, of rain

we crouch to crawl in
the oldest darkest
of our temples,
each chosen stone
carried with deliberation
to the rite place

floating the pap
on the long ridge,
shaping the chamber
for ashes, arrowheads,
burnt bone and
the encrypted urn

such things as were
intended to be seen
when the slab was lifted,
after a mound of time
the rickle of boulders
is still sound

we take turns
to creep the passage
into the paved womb
– Rhodri's plucked harp-strings
fall in and out of silence

shifting the tone,
throwing a thousand,
thousand images
buoyed into the light,
where they reverberate
off flecked gneiss

we hug our knees
tighter together
in the chamber,
sensing the dark
as a membrane
of time

feeling silence within,
before we arrive,
after we leave,
squaring the circle
of longing,
reconciling the need

for distance
and the desire
for settledness,

for what's an ending
but the place
you begin again

*Bashō's Nezu Barrier
is our Berneray
we cross the causeway from Uist
to the hostel at Baile*

*the spirit of the place
recalling the old sisters
Annie and Jessie
crofters and wardens*

Berneray –
aye, Berneray.
Berneray!

how many folk were offered
their scones, pancake spreads
and strawberry jam
with the lilting refrain

*very good
very good*

windbent in faded blue macs
herding the sheep
with their handbags
shearing them by hand

Annie's place isn't right
for us to come in
but she'll sit a while
with us at the door

her hands are shaky
but she's still the wit
to gently tease

   Eck, are you not married yet?

every time I visit
I get something new,
this time it's the memory
of those who've died

   Jessie gone
   & Angus
   & Rover
   & Kirsty too

grey though it is
there's pearl
gleaming to the west
over the far beach

and I've this elegy
to record, for Kirsty,
where we made love
in the dunes

where I snapped her
after a dip *(so kalt!)*,
wearing nothing
but one of the sisters'

enormous
thick cable-knit
aquamarine
jumpers

X

Crossing into Autumn

a walk to the summit of Slioch, Wester Ross

departing geese
and the foxgloves
not yet over

the groves of Isle Maree, Wester Ross

this sylvan reliquary
of native and naturalised
binds species together
in polyphony

Druidic oak and
rowan commune
with saintly holly
and Viking larch

on the deer path in
from the shingle beach
through myrtle and blaeberry
we praise them all

willow and dog-rose
birch and juniper
chestnut and sycamore
alder and beech

the heads and half-moons
of copper coins
feeing silent hopes
in the wishing tree

and cut into bark
about the well
a heart pierced through
with an arrow

by graves within stones
we pour a libation
on the carved crosses
of the Viking lovers

unfurling a black sail
unfolding a white shroud

sharing *pain of one who goes*
emptiness of one left behind

*a walk part-way up, part-way down,
the River Inverianvie, Wester Ross*

pulling my legs
along with my eyes,
drawing a straight line

in-between grey-
clitched boulders
and tarry puddles

walk on, walk on,
when your boots
get bent

walk on, walk on,
to the white noise
of the waterfall

walk on, walk on,
with a dream
of the lochan

walk on, walk on,
as far as the name-
less glen

walk on, walk on,
kist beneath Carn
an Lochain Dubh

walk on, walk on,
sensing skyline
after skyline

walk on, walk on,
anticipating every
bend of the river

walk on, walk on,
this far, this close,
to the water

walk on, walk on,
part-way up Inverianvie,
or part-way down

walk on, walk on,
wherever we are now
I can go no further

looking back
down the path
to the sea

letting go the loch
I pour the tea
thinking of dear Tom

still giving illumination
as language flickered
and dimmed

poetry is still beautiful

taking me with it

quiet but still something

ground, river and sea

my body my tree

after that it becomes simply the world

accepting the mountains
may remain
too high

reeling in the grip
of exhaustion
I nod to the two climbers
descending from An Teallach

as they pass
sullen with exhaustion
I ask

>   *been in far?*
>   *four days*

I'm too shy to say,

>   *what did you see?*
>   *how bad was the weather?*

now I've to find
my way out this glen,
back by the waterfall

leaving my wishes to
walk on, walk on,
over the next rise

walk on, walk on,
around the next bend
to Loch a' Mhadaidh Mòr

Glen Etive

now wet summer's given
way to autumn sun
we approach from the north
below Stobh a' Ghlais Choire
kayakers plunge the white waters
to a freezing pool

the road-map builds
a string of villages
where on the ground
there's less than
a few scattered houses
guarded by brute geese

we pick three tawny pips
from a ripe red apple
for the three sons of Uisneach
poking finger-holes
in the peaty ooze
wetted by Allt Fhaolain

in the lee of a rock
among rowan and birch
for arbours and ardours
we plant three apple seeds
for the love of
the three brothers

the lochside tideline
tangles holly and alder
twigs and Nikes
by Sora's damp beacon
Mrs Climber tells us
the Buachaille is her lover

has been for years
she came up late last night
but the Great Herdsman
bumped her off and today
she's obliged to return
south to city streets

XI

Winter Interned

Sora's illness is Alec's Long Winter Illness

night's cave
is made
from the inside

when the tide is high
take the path through
   the graves

my shanks grow thin
as long as they
   still climb

expect me Yosimo
in cherry blossom
   time

XII

Weak March Sun

what is a hut?

a hut is four thin walls
nailed around a stove
set in woods, wilds

or at the back of a garden
where it grows organically
as a collage of accretion,
borrowing, make-do-and-mending

*Bashō's Butcho-osho
is Gerry Loose & Morven Gregor*

*his Unganji
is their hut at Carbeth
where the deer path leads past the door
and the roof has moss for rafters*

it's just a wee felt-roofed hut,
a shame to stay inside
but there is rain,
wisps of white smoke
rising straightforwardly
from the chimley,
yaffles trying to laugh
their way in

weak March sun
sups the sap's tonicity,
there's lovage and angelica
– too strong tasting
for deer or rabbits –
and last year's tansy
buttons that fashion
this spring's brown

Dumgoyach's a few steps away
but I'll just sit on this log
drinking smoky tea
and wait for the windfalls,
so's I can roll
their weight in my hand,
hold their bruises
away from me

XIII

Spring Paths and Summer Opening

what is faith?

the confluence
of burn with river
river with sea

a dandelion
awaiting a favourable wind
to blow across Alba

the ivy
that holds up
the wall

a bell
that rings
the silence

a name opened
to reveal the hidden
seed of its meaning

a path walked
with eyes shut
or open

Alec's path to St Medan's Cave and Chapel, Luce Bay

I chose my narrow way
marked by flowers and birdsong

I plunged down the dragon's back ridge
in search of the seaside cell

I did penance for my haste
kneeling on a tussocky knoll

I was trapped for an hour
in the gentle pastorage

I clambered back over cliffs
found my way about the point
up through a chimney of rock

I lay down in a rich sea-meadow
suitable for spiritual growth

I restated my creed of sprawl and loll
christening this terraqueous ecosystem

  Medana

The Lesson

I ask myself
if I had patiently sought
melliferous orchid, tormentil,
primroses, gorse and ferns,
bluebells, meadowsweet and thrift
might I have found the chapel
tucked away among the rocks?

Ken's path to St Medan's Cave and Chapel, Luce Bay

I stayed longer on the high road
of the gorse path

I descended seeking a structure
among eroded cliffs

I speculated which rock
might be her schooner

I marked in red
for 'cassock' read 'tussock'
for 'saint' read 'snail'

I consoled myself
for a mystery withheld
in summer flora

I found the stones
when I'd stopped seeking

I smelled the air
heavy with star-white ramsons

I looked into the darkness
of her chosen retreat

I wondered when the mist
hiding the far shore
would lift

Bashō's cascade known as Urami Falls
are the Falls at Acharn viewed from The Hermitage

today of all days
our last on the *hosomichi*
seeking Bashō's view

we left our car behind
climbing perhaps
a quarter of a mile

up a last steep path
fringed by shady groves
gean, hazel and larch

and a young beech
holding on to the old
until it's sure of the new

guessed by the sound
that we were near the cascade
but could not see it

entered a dungeon
-like passage and
after walking some yards

in total darkness
found ourselves in
a quaint apartment

ornamented with
a library of books
covered with old leather backs

mock hermit furniture
not for reading
their being wooden

and as we emerged from
this theatrical cave
the view was

upstaged by a red
squirrel scampering
into our attention

and then we saw
the white rush of falls
across the gorge

through a large bow-
window and looking
down to the left

the village of Kenmore
and a part of the lake
a very beautiful prospect

in the gap
between beeches
over pools and tresses

only for a time
to a waterfall confined
summer opening

XIV

Epilogues

Alec's Epilogue

would we could
live our lives
as a novel
read backwards

secure in our ending
as a tied rope
or taut stay
each strand untwisting

a moment
tense with shock
giddy for joy
when love becomes

our delirious ending
we slowly un-wind
to the tight knot
of that familiar

difficult beginning
would we could glimmer
the perfect form
of an idea

emerging complete
in its own right
from out some vague
insubstantial object

only every now
and then we may
be brave enough to dare
a handstand

emptying out our
pockets, seeing
inside a world
turned upside-down

Ken's Epilogue

Whether it was planning or
our hearts doing
the right thing,
on the last day
we found our way
to my sister Judy
in the fold of Killin

finding the right shampoo
that fits you
and no more tears

finding a haircut
that suits you
or a wig

finding something
to wear
that goes

finding a view
that you can cling to
then opening the window

finding a journey
to make
and the right map

finding a pair of sticks
that fit your stride
and a walk

finding how not to
contradict the path
and end up with sore legs

finding the healing
that heals you
and a good doctor

finding a flat
with space enough for
company and solitude

finding a tea
the best cup
deserves

finding a hill
that's fine in sunshine
or wrapped in mist

finding a chocolate
so good
you eat only a little

finding an answer
so wrong
you rewrite the question

finding a coat
that fits so well
you long for winter

finding a spring
near the shore
dabbling against the breakers

finding that if the heart
is a valve
then the heart's also a bell

finding a language
in which you feel
at home

finding a life
that fulfils you
and a death too

Appendix

stations, teas and whiskies

at each of our 54 stations we shared and libated a tea and a whisky

1. Edo (Edinburgh): Gabalong Black & Nikka White
2. Ueno (Falkland): Tie Guan Yin (Monkey on the Mountain) & Auchentoshan
3. Soka (Kinloch-Rannoch): Heather tea & The Blend of Nikka
4. Muro-no-Yashima (Isle of Boreray): Wuyi Red Robe Oolong & Lagavulin
5. Mt. Nikko (Slioch): Curly-winged Silver Dragon & Nikka Pure Malt Red
6. Toshogu (Achnabreck): Buddha's Hand Foshou Hon Cha & Isle of Arran
7. Mt. Kurokami (Killin & Acharn): Tea of Life & Tomatin
8. Kurobane (Loch Insh): Goomtee White Ball Darjeeling & Dalwhinnie
9. Nasu (Monreith): Moroccan Mint & Bladnoch
10. Unganji (Carbeth): Summer Green Tea & Glengoyne
11. Sesshoseki (Tingwall): Yunnan Imperial & Nikka from the Barrel
12. Ashino (Aberfeldy): Emperor Jiaqing (Old Tree Phoenix Oolong) & Ledaig (1993)
13. Shirakawa no Seki (Sma' Glen): Oriental Beauty - Bai Hao & Glenturret (10 years old)
14. Kagenuma (St Fillan's Hill): Jasmine Hei Cha & Glenturret (8 years old)
15. Sukagawa (Dalchonzie & Dunira): Yonnan & Tullibardine (1993)
16. Kurozuka (Ossian's Cave): Liquorice pink & Aberfeldy
17. Shinobu (Kilmartin): Yun Ti Kuan Yin Ta & Islay Mist
18. Mt. Maruyama (Dun Carloway): Himifuuki Japanese black tea & Aberlour (10 years old)
19. Iizuka (Munlochy): Osmanthus Black & Glenmorangie
20. Abumizuri (Glenelg): Hei Cha Hunan Dark Tea & An Cnoc
21. Takekuma (Dunkeld & Birnam): Liquorice pink & Edradour (Dougie Maclean)
22. Miyagi (Crarae): Master Wang's 'Old Peach Nut' – Guan Dong & Glen Scotia
23. Tsubo no Ishibumi (Glen Lyon): Silver Tips & Deanston
24. Sue-no-Matsuyama (Sand Chapel, Gruinard Bay): Black Spiral & Penderyn

25. Shiogama Myojin (Dunsinane): Grasshopper Oolong & Super Nikka
26. Ojima (Isle of Luing): Buddha Mt. Dao Ren & Yamazaki
27. Ungozenji (Sandaig): Huiming Temple Gold & Speyburn
28. Zuiganji (Jupiter Artland): Keemun Black Tiger & Glenkinchie
29. Hiraizumi (Isle of Hoy): Puerh (Yunnan Chitsu Pingcha) & Highland Park
30. Izumi (Dunstaffnage & Beregonium): Black Mao Hou Monkey Fur & Ledaig (1990)
31. Shitomae (Ben Dorain): Iron Buddha Oolong & Nikka All Malt
32. Dewa (Huntly): Peaceful Monkey King & Glenfiddich
33. Obanazawa (St Weems): Rose-flavoured Hei Cha dark tea & Aberlour
34. Ryushakuji (Outlandia): Rou Gui Oolong & Dew of Ben Nevis
35. Shiraito (Falls of Bruar): Black Ruby & Edradour (1997)
36. Mt. Haguroyama (Schiehallion): Little Dragon Long Jing & Tullibardine (1992)
37. Mt. Gassan (Loch Etive) Yunnan Imperial & Springbank
38. Tsuru-ga-oka (Glen Fruin): Liu An Guapian & Nikka Pure Black Malt
39. Noin (Isle of Raasay): Ali Shan Taiwan Oolong (10 years old) & Poit Dubh
40. Nezu (Isle of Bernerary): Assam Night Jasmine & Mac Na Mara
41. Komagaeeshi (Rhenigidale): Jasmine Chung Hao & Tobermory
42. Kurobe (Inverianvie): Jun Shan Golden Needle & Old Pulteney
43. Mt. Unohana (Loch Ruthven): Hong Shui Red Oolong & Laphroig
44. Komatsu (Dunadd): Japanese Cherry Tea & Caol Ila
45. Mt. Shirane (The Quirang): King of Ginseng & Talisker
46. Yamanka (Loch Maree): Phoenix Honey Orchid B & Ardbeg
47. Zenshoji (Stonypath & Brownsbank): Iron Warrior Monk Tie Luo Han & Glen Dronach
48. Shiogoshi (Loch Eilt): Gyokuro Organic & Cú Dhub
49. Eiheiji (Langais): Rou Gui & Té Bheag
50. Fukui (Kilmiddlefern): Wintertime Tea of Life & Oban
51. Tsuruga (Tarskavaig): Keemun Black Tiger & Bruichladdich
52. Iro (Loch Ailort): Summertime Tea of Life & Isle of Jura
53. Ogaki (the hidden gardens): various teas & gean brandy
54. Epilogue: Keemun Hao Ya & Nikka White

Notes and Acknowledgements

Bashō (1644–1694) travelled through northern Honshu (the main Japanese island) in 1689 with his companion Sora. *Oku-no-hosomichi* was written in 1692–3. It is a short book, often divided into chapters or 'stations' by location: Corman's and Susuke's version gives 53 'stations', plus the epilogue by the calligrapher Soryū.

The idea of translating Bashō and Sora's journey to Scotland was first conceived by Alec Finlay in 1999.

Neither of us speak Japanese, but we picked up a few words along the way.

oku is the north country, the highlands, the out-of-the-way-places.
hosomichi are the B-roads, single-track roads and farm tracks you use to get there.
Edo – our Edinburgh – is where they're not: the capital city in Bashō's time, renamed Tokyo in 1868.
tanzaku are strips of paper used for writing poems on, and the word has come to mean 'poem'; our translation was the poem-label.
nadokoro are 'places of name', rich with associations.

The River Inerianvie poem includes some lines from the memoir *Until Further Notice, I Am Alive* by Tom Lubbock (1957–2011). The Acharn Falls includes extracts from Dorothy Wordsworth's diary from September 1803.

Our thanks go to the following poets who recollected, visited and wrote about the stations we were unable to visit:

Ian Stephen (Isle of Boreray)
Jen Hadfield (Tingwall)
Linda France (Crarae Garden)
Alistair Peebles (Isle of Hoy)
Colin Will (Ben Dorain)
Morven Gregor, Gerry Loose and Peter Manson (Glen Fruin).

We would also like to thank those who shared the road north with us:

Rebecca Hall, Paul Edgerley, Luke Allan, Grazyna Fremi and Larissa Hamilton, Angus, Mark and Tana Reid, Sonia Ferras-Mana, The

Administrator, Ian Stephen, Nick Thompson, Lorna Irvine and Holly Hayward, Isobel Cockburn, Judy Holden, Jon Thomson and Alison Craighead, Margaret Bennett and Gonzalo Mazzei, Jon Macleod, Angus Dunn, Eddie Stiven, Kevin Henderson, Norrie Bissell, Edna Whyte, Robert and Nicky Wilson, Alice Ladenburg, Claudia Zeiske, Anna Vermehren, Norma Hunter, Jayne Wilding, Bruce Gilchrist and Jo Joelson, Donald and Maisie Cockburn, Meg Bateman, Eilidh Crumlish and Geoff Lucas, Maoilios and Margaret Caimbeul, Jerome Rothenberg, all at Taigh Chearsabhagh, Andy McKinnon, Rhodri Davies and Angharad Closs, Annie Briggs, Malcolm Fraser and Helen Lucas, all at the Hidden Gardens, Irfan Merchant, Momus.

Parts of *the road north* have appeared (sometimes as variants of the texts here) in the publications and on the websites below, and our thanks go to their editors:

a-ga: on mountains, Les Citadelles, Northwords Now, Shearsman, Sunfish, Stravaig, The Apple Anthology, The Art of Walking: A Field Guide.

Extracts also appeared on *Resonance FM* and *Literaturtelefon Kiel*, and were published on the following blogs by Alec Finlay: *Sweeney's Bothy* and *Dukes Wood*.

The complete blog of *the road north* is available online: www.theroadnorth.co.uk

A recording of the poem, *the road north*, performed by Ken Cockburn, Alec Finlay and Lila Matsumoto, with lever harp by Rhodri Davies and sound design by Geoff Sample, is available as a free download from iTunes at https://itunes.apple.com/gb/podcast/road-north-alec-finlay-ken/id907451517?mt=2&uo=4. Use the QR code on the following page for quick access.

the road north also exists as an archival artwork, exhibited at the Scottish Poetry Library, Edinburgh (2011); StAnza, St Andrews (2012); and as part of the touring exhibition Walk On (2013-14).

Ken Cockburn
Alec Finlay
Edinburgh, July 2014

www.ingramcontent.com/pod-product-compliance
Lightning Source LLC
Chambersburg PA
CBHW031152160426
43193CB00008B/339